All Scripture references taken from the KJV of the Bible unless otherwise indicated.

The Abundance of Jesus

by Dr. Marlene Miles

Freshwater Press 2024

ISBN: 978-1-963164-84-8

Paperback Version

Table of Contents

The Abundance of Jesus

Freshwater

Freshwater Press

Abundance

Abundance means having plenty; ample sufficiency and in my opinion more than enough and a fullness of whatever is being quantified. *Abundance* refers to tangible things as well as intangible things such as an *Abundance* of happiness, joy, or compassion, for example. A person may have an *Abundance* of knowledge or Wisdom; it is not always about money.

The *abundance* of the rich is great wealth, (Ecclesiastes 5:10)

Jesus came that we may have life and have it more abundantly. If you are not having life and having it more abundantly there may be something, or a lot of things wrong. I picture the promises of Psalm 91 as a major part of having an abundant life, but God is so amazing, that I'm sure that is not all. Protection, no fear, dwell in safety, deliverance from attacks and all evil, no fear of death, even witchcraft and occultic arrows won't hit you. That's amazing too, since arrows were even shot at Joseph in the Old Testament. The abundant life is described throughout the Bible, but in our example, Psalm 91 continues with, Angels will have watch over you so nothing will happen to you, you won't even dash your foot on a rock. When you fight enemies, you will win, they will fall, but you won't. We shall be saved, and God will be with us, and we can live a long time. I like to say, live until we are satisfied. Amen. That is an abundant life.

We must clarify, you will not have **Abundance** just because Jesus came, but you must accept Him as your Lord and Savior and you are *all in* Christ.

Let's sort it out, further.

Expecting Jesus

After being overshadowed by the Holy Spirit, Mary had firsthand knowledge of what was about to transpire, but she wasn't the only one expecting Jesus. People were expecting Jesus – for years, decades, even centuries.

Jesus was both expected in the New Testament and prophesied about and also *seen* in the Old Testament. He **Was** and **Is** and **Is to Come**; only Jesus can do and be all that. The Scriptures speak of a mysterious priest-king, Melchisedek. When the Messiah comes, He will have a priesthood derived from Melchizedek's (not from the Levitical priesthood):

You are a priest forever in the order of Melchizedek (Psalm 110:4b).

Melchizedek, the King of Salem is a foreshadowing of Jesus. Melchizedek is described as being without ancestry, without beginning of days or end of life. (Hebrews 7). This writer believes that Melchizedek is a vision of Christ pre-incarnate, without earthly father, mother, or ancestry, without beginning of days or end of life. This could only be the Lord!

This brings clarity to why Abraham paid tithes to Him. The text says that He was made to *resemble* Christ, so, we surmise that Melchizedek is a *type* or prefigurate image of Christ. There are types and foreshadows of Christ all through the Old Testament, but there are certain appearances in the OT, that I believe are Christ, ***Himself.***

This writer also believes that the appearance of Melchizedek and Abraham's paying tithes to him is a parenthetical vision, like many in the Book of Revelation. I believe that what it is a vision of is Abraham paying tithes, 10% of all and the vision of that altar that Abraham established, interfacing the natural with the spiritual realm. Abraham's sacrifice was not only *received* in the Spirit, the image of Christ, as the King of Salem came down **personally** and accepted it. The Bible shows us this transaction in the Spirit, in words.

Jesus is our Great Intercessor. He receives our sacrifices and uses them to worship the Father on our behalf.

Abraham had gotten the money from spoils of battle with these kings to rescue his nephew, Lot, in Genesis 14. Abraham paid that tithe thereby sanctifying those gains. My Bible doesn't show another account of Abraham being involved in a war after he paid that tithe and made covenant with God.

The Lord will also reprove kings for your sake. Abraham went and got his nephew Lot who had been captured by pagan forces. That was very shepherd-like--, it is as a warring shepherd would do. Abraham's victory over them shows God's reproval of these monarchs.

The Word says that Jesus, our Good Shepherd will leave the 99 to go get the one. And, if you are His, and in relationship with Him, He will come and get you if you are lost or captured.

I don't think it was a coincidence that Abraham waited 99 years for the one, the child of Promise--, Isaac.

Jesus will also wait for and come and get the one. See how He has drawn us with cords of lovingkindness for years and years until we finally see Him and accept Him. For some, it is all their life that Jesus is waiting, never giving up on a man who is called and chosen. That lost man might be 99 years old but once he accepts Christ, just as the man on the cross by Jesus, that saved man can now *enter in*to paradise. Jesus is the Good Shepherd, but like David, He is a warring shepherd, battling for his flock and what is *His*.

Afterward Abraham sanctified the money he got, but he also paid it to the King of Salem, and *salem* means *peace*. Look at Abraham's love for and dedication to Lot, that he would go to war for him, that he would fight five kings for him, and then give of the spoils, that is pay money for Lot. We can see God in all this and that the ransom He gave for us, even after all the fighting and battling, was Jesus Christ. Amen.

The author of Hebrews declares Melchizedek's priesthood to be far superior to the Levitical order because He obviously was a higher and greater altar than Abraham since Abraham *tithed* to Him. Could this be why so few tithe? They either have a wrong relationship with Mammon, or they don't know what an altar is. Or, could it be that they don't see the altar where they are as a greater altar than they themselves? The altar at the church they attend is not a greater altar to them than the mall?

Further this King of Salem lives forever; as said He was and He Is and He Is to Come. Tithes are paid to a higher altar; that is why it is so foolish for a Christian to not discern the altar they are sacrificing on. Especially if a Christian steps to a demonic altar to sacrifice or offer sacrifice on it, they are demoting themselves.

Altars are forever, unless God or someone speaking for God destroys that altar. Therefore, an altar *was, is,* and unless it is stopped, it also *is to come*. Jesus cannot be stopped, but lesser and evil altars can be discontinued, burned up, and torn down.

There's a Fourth Man in the fire with the three Hebrew boys in the Book of Daniel, and His name is Jesus, Emmanuel, God with us. This was another Old Testament appearance of Jesus. Jesus **Was**, **He Is**, and **He Is to Come**.

So Jacob was left alone, and a
man wrestled with him till daybreak.
Genesis 32:24

Two men are walking along the road to Emmaus after the crucifixion of our Lord and Savior, Jesus Christ. A third man approached them, and they walked and talked together. Did God not come down into the Garden of Eden in the cool of the day and talk with two? Adam & Eve, until they sinned and hid. Jesus did what He saw His Father do. Jesus fulfilled the Old Testament. Some Bible scholars say He fulfilled as many as 300 Old Testament prophecies.

On that road, these two men didn't hide. They didn't hide physically, nor did they hide their hearts or their beliefs but continued to speak of the life of Jesus Christ to this third man. What do you say about Christ when you think He is not present? What do you say even to others when you think Jesus is not listening? Do you act the clown? Do you speak unbelief? Do you seek after mischief?

The two men on the Road to Emmaus even postured that Jesus Christ might be alive because His tomb was found empty. Do you tell others in your words and deeds that Jesus is alive? You must because they may think He is dead--, that He was crucified and that was the end of that. No, He's not dead!

When the men get to Emmaus and begin to have supper, the Third Man is recognized as Jesus himself as He broke and blessed the bread. Saints of God, can you be recognized by your *spiritual signature*? Can you be recognized by your prayer style? Can you be recognized by the words you speak and how you minister to others? Jesus could; Jesus can. With relationship, experience and discernment you can know when God is speaking and when it is a phony or an imposter, by Jesus' Spirit, by His spiritual signature, by His style. Blessed is he who believes, yet has not seen. They recognized Him by the way He walked, talked, and by the way He prayed and broke that bread.

My sheep know my voice; the voice of another they will not follow. (John 10:27)

When the two men realized it was Jesus they went back to Jerusalem to announce His resurrection and the fact that He Lives!

If your salvation is sure and your prayer life is solid, then won't the spirit world recognize that even if in the past sin killed you spiritually, even though rebellion and disobedience tried to pull you into hell that you also now live in Christ? Even though life tried to beat you down, don't you know that in your Salvation in Christ, **you** have been resurrected also? You were spiritually dead in sin; and now *in Christ* you live again. Don't you know that the tomb the devil had for you is empty and will remain so, in the Name of Jesus?

Prophecies of Messiah

Not just Mary was expecting Jesus. The coming of Messiah had been prophesied for hundreds of years before Mary was with child--, before Mary was ever born.

Those prophecies from the Bible include, but are not limited to the following:

Messiah would be born of a woman. (Genesis 3:15).

Messiah would be born in Bethlehem. (Micah 5:2)

Messiah would be born of a virgin. (Isaiah 7:14)

Messiah will come from the lineage of Abraham, Isaac, and Jacob. (Genesis 12:3)

Messiah would come from the Tribe of Judah. (Genesis 49:10)

Messiah would be heir to David's Throne. (Isaiah 9:7)

And His name shall be called, Emmanuel, God with us. (Isaiah)

Messiah will be declared the Son of God. (Psalm 2:7)

Messiah will heal the brokenhearted. (Isaiah 61:1-2)

Messiah will be called King. (Psalm 2:6)

Messiah would be seated at God's right hand. (Psalm 68:18)

Messiah would be a sacrifice for sin. (Isaiah 53:5-12)

Messiah would return a second time. (Daniel 7:13-14)

When someone is prophesied about it is because they are important. When they are important to a family, a region, a nation, or the entire world, there may be many prophecies recorded about them. Jesus was spiritually important, so many prophecies are recorded about Him in the Bible. All were not listed above. In order to fulfill prophecies, prophecies had to have already existed before Christ. And they would have been prophesied and spoken and respoken and carried and believed and expected.

The Star of Bethlehem

Can anything good come out of Nazareth? Can anything good come out of Bethlehem? That Star over Bethlehem said that something great could come out of it. However, because that was asked it could have been a sarcastic question or an objective question since maybe nothing good had ever come out of Nazareth before. Historically perhaps all 200 people, which was the population of Nazareth at the time of Jesus' birth, were suppressed from greatness or renown of any kind.

Was there spiritual suppression, as in territorial powers or was there natural dog-eat-dog, crabs in a barrel mentality amongst the people there? *Was it both?* Is this why people from Nazareth did not excel? Perhaps there was just no opportunity to excel.

Saying, Where is he that is born King of the Jews? for we have seen his star in the east, and are come to worship him.(Mathew 2:2)

Jesus had a magnificent Star because He had A LOT of work to do.

For unto whomsoever much is given, of him shall be much required: and to whom men have committed much, of him they will ask the more. (Luke 12:48b)

Was His Star visible to everyone or were the astrologers and star hunters the only ones looking for it? If the Magi traveled 2.5 years to reach the child to bring Him gifts and worship Him, then the Star had to have remained in place all that time for their navigation purposes. It had to be outstanding and magnificent. You'd have to almost pay somebody to make you not see that Star.

What was given in Jesus' Star?

MUCH. The magnitude of a man's star portends his successes, victories, wealth. Three wise men, the Magi brought Jesus very pricey baby shower gifts because they saw that Star.

Were the three wise men unctioned by GOD, and or moved by the Star, as to the location? The magnitude of the Star confirmed who just came to Earth; the Star *led* them.

__Your__ **star** should lead your wise men to you. Your wise men are your destiny helpers, they are your benefactors, they are your divine connections, pastors, ministers, your teachers and even your healthcare providers, should you need them. In your star is your spouse, your marriage and your sexual rights, and eventually your children at the appointed time in your life. In your star is your education, career, ministry, your health and your wealth.

Your divine timeline is in your star.

For I know the plans I have for you, plans
of a future and an expected end.
(Jeremiah 29:11)

For I come in the volume of the book that
it is written of me. (Psalm 40)

Mariners use stars to navigate their boats and ships. Astronomers know what stars are where, and they know when new stars are born. Those new stars are discovered. In the natural, astronomers study the stars, but spiritually, astrologers are the stargazers and the star-studiers. Those astrologers can be on the side of darkness if they are looking for stars to steal, hide, mask, cover, or do other nefarious things to them.

The Wise Men saw the star and they came to worship. *Wise men* was a euphemism for astrologer or diviner in Bible days.

The gifts the Wise Men gave were appropriate for *their* station in life, or appropriate for a Star of that magnitude. They came to worship a **king**, because that was a King's STAR.

The average star – what must that be like? What does God put in it? What does God give to everyman? It depends on what the spiritual purpose and destiny of that *every man* should be. To whom much is given, much is required. Conversely, to whom much is required God appropriates appropriate gifts and graces them with a commensurate star.

That you have a star is pretty impressive, actually.

The *Other* Wise Men

The gifts of God allotted to you are in your star. The gifts of God are given without repentance; they must be, else they wouldn't be gifts. This, however, means that the gifts that a person has can be used for the Kingdom of God, be dormant and not used at all, or misused in the kingdom of darkness. The first is desirable, the latter two are sin.

When you are using your gifts for the Kingdom of Heaven, this affords you protection against many intruders and interlopers. Herein lies some of that *Abundance*, some of that protection by God--, when you are doing what you are supposed to be doing, spiritually, and otherwise. In the natural, it's kind of like, if you are driving your car at 60 miles an hour, it is hard for someone to jack your vehicle.

If you are parked in your fine vehicle, sitting in a park having a drink or a smoke, anyone could walk up and take your car from you. Saints of God, it is when you are NOT working your gifts that they can be stolen.

Additionally, Herod had his own soothsayers and *wise men* who may have also told him that this Star was very important and destiny changing. Kings were known to have spiritual advisors and sometimes an *Abundance* of them. Pharaoh had *"wisemen"* in his court. Nebuchadnezzar had wise men too, but none of those diviners, which are actually false prophets could tell or interpret either of those king's dreams.

Diviners and false prophets get their information from the second heaven, and it is usually secondhand information along with guess work, where they bait you with a few words, they tell you something that makes you tell them the rest. Divination information is usually of the past, fortune teller type information is usually lies and false. Magic tricks; but time tells it all. (Thank you, *Time*.)

It is possible that Herod's evil wisemen knew that there was a magnificent star in the skies. They could have been scoping out stars to steal, or Herod could have had them on assignment. Hey, this Star was in the East, and they were in the East— this king, this new king, this *other* king--, someone of tremendous importance must be nearby. I bet Herod freaked out with that knowledge. Herod's wise men either told him, **That's a King's star** or the fact that Wise Men were coming to see this Star carried importance. Or that three wisemen, The Magi were coming showed the weight of this glory. In addition, if they knew what the Wisemen had in their caravan as gifts, this would have been indicative of the greatness of who they were coming to worship, as well.

But, if there was prophecy after prophecy for centuries even, do we think that only *three* wise men would notice the coming of this great King and see His Star?

If Herod was the kind of king that we may think he was, evil, insecure, and covetous of his power and position then if he saw what those gifts were and that the Wise Men didn't bring Herod a gift at all, or gifts of a similar level, could have also been part of what incensed him? If so, how childish—, Herod it's not *your* birthday.

Folks, there is *Abundance* in every star, but Jesus's Star? There was **major** *Abundance* in that Star.

He Came from Heaven to Earth

What Jesus left in Heaven to come here to save us was incredible by Earth standards. He became *poor* for our sakes – financially poor? Physically poor? Folks, money is not an issue unless you either don't have any, and/or you worship it. Money is a by-product of life, in a sense. You need it, you earn it, you make it, you use it; you share it. You leave it when you leave Earth and until that time, you don't worship it. Trust this, you won't worship wealth, riches and *Abundance* in Heaven, but you will be surrounded by it.

Do you think the devil or any of his prison guards in hell are asking for money or bribes to stop the constant torment that its victims are subject to? Of course, not; the devil has already ripped that sinner off to the max before death, plus all forms of currency and things of Earth value would be completely consumed in hell fires anyway.

So now we have proved that currency, silver, gold, diamonds, bitcoin--, none of that will be needed in the afterlife--, neither the *upper* or the *lower* afterlife.

Therefore, to keep your eyes on things eternal, leaning on the Word and works of God, **Abundance** will come. Speaking of true riches, it is not about money or just money. Money is a natural indication of **Abundance**. John the Baptist and Jesus were both born Spirit-filled. Gifts of the Spirit are strong indicators of *true wealth*.

But the angel said to him: "Do not be afraid, Zechariah; your prayer has been heard. Your wife Elizabeth will bear you a son, and you are to call him John. for he will be great in the sight of the Lord. He is never to take wine or other fermented drink, and he will be filled with the Holy Spirit even before he is born. (Luke 1:13, 15)

You've heard people say that sometimes others act like they've never had anything in their life or seen anything in

28

their life before. Folks with money and *Abundance* and have put that money in its place, behave themselves well when they are around it.

Those who don't have and may not have ever had, grew up poor, for example, may talk about money and things of value incessantly. They may brag. They may worry about it, or become paranoid about who wants to steal from them. They may not be wrong because people do steal and will even become your fake friend to steal from you in any number of ways. But we don't fret over the evil doings of sinners, criminals, and thieves. Instead, we are wise and stay prayed up.

So, this star of great importance and great *Abundance* found it's place in the sky and held that place for Jesus until He had need of it, used it, and returned to Glory at the appointed time. That star guides that person, that star empowers that man. That star. As we sojourn here, are we like mariners in a sense that the stars – specifically our star guides us? We don't worship stars, we don't listen to the words of astrologers because their information is divination. But, our God-given star is necessary for a successful destiny, so we cannot afford to lose it.

1. Lord, let me know the Abundance of Sufficiency as it pertains to money and all things involving life and Godliness, in the Name of Jesus.

OT Joseph's Star

Joseph's ten older brothers didn't see Joseph's star in the natural, although they potentially could have since they were all alive when Joseph was born. Were they too flesh-involved to look up at the stars? Were they ignorant of how to stargaze? The people from Ur, were astrologers. Joseph's great-grandfather, Abraham had been an astrologer before he was saved by Faith and entered into covenant with Jehovah, but maybe all that idolatry was purged out of the bloodline by the times of Jacob's kids, so looking up at the stars may not have been a thing to them anymore.

One would hope so, but it probably wasn't. In Genesis, one day Jacob's daughter, Dinah went out to see the girls of the land --, that is she went out to do some idol worship and ended up being attacked and captured and taken by her rapist.

So, at least one of this family hadn't fully given up the idolatry that was in their bloodline.

When the pendulum swings too far one may forget natural knowledge because your spiritual knowledge takes over. I have a sister who does not at this time profess Christ, but she is full of knowledge, life's experiences, and common sense. I pray for her Salvation in Christ, but I don't expect that she'll lose any brain cells or memories in the process. Amen. Those of us who are in Christ cannot forget where we came from or the experiences and knowledge that we gained from going *through*, even in the world. Sometimes it is why we went *through*, so when we got saved, we could still relate to others and help others out of similar situations.

Dinah, didn't anyone ever tell you to stop chasing after idols? Oh, they did, but you didn't listen? Did you see what happened to other idolaters? Why did you think nothing would happen to you? Oh, you thought the idols would protect you, so you just did what you've always done?

Until we are fully *in Christ* and converted, what is in our familial blood will simply call out to us in a sense and program our actions. Sometimes those actions are the same sins that our ancestors committed.

Balance. We must remember where we come from, and come from there to progress in life, naturally and spiritually. None of us should be so much in the flesh that we are of no spiritual good. And, none of us should be so spiritual, that we are of no earthly good.

Jacob's Star

Let's talk about Jacob's star. Jacob was the second born of Isaac's and Rebecca's twins who I believe **STOLE** his brother, Esau's firstborn *birthright*. The Bible account says that Esau SOLD his birthright for the porridge when he was so hungry he thought he'd die of starvation. So, Esau sold his birthright – his star or his destiny for food.

If that weren't enough, then Jacob went on to trick his father out of the blessing of the firstborn when Jacob was about to transition out of this world.

Folks' deathbed confessions and blessings are serious. So many cultures and people still pay attention to what the old people, the wise ones, the dying say, confess, and instruct them to do at the last moments of Earth life.

But should they?

Not all people on their deathbeds are in their right minds; some are even on very strong painkillers, so what they say if you know they are not sane and sober should be judged against the Word of God and straight up commonsense.

One sundowning and transitioning old woman had dying words for her 40+ year old children. The son, she told to take care of his sister and told her daughter to cook for and take care of her brother. Basically, from their hearing and understanding, even though they were both married at the time, this old woman married them to one another and since she's been dead for 20+ years neither of the two of them can stay in a marriage. At this time, they have left matrimonial homes and now live together, heading into their old age. For the last two decades if either of them got into a serious relationship, somehow the other would break it up.

Demonic instructions, even from well-meaning folks, leads to disaster in the natural. You don't think that the dying can be used by the devil? Think again.

Before she was deathly ill, that deceased woman had a meltdown on an airplane and took off all her clothes. Now that she is dead, she has gone on to another realm and has no recall or awareness of what she did to two marriages, several grandchildren, by *marrying* her two children to each other, which is incest.

This is what she left in her wake. I guess a wake is called a wake for more than one reason.

Back to Isaac and Jacob and Esau: if hungry-Esau didn't sell his star to Jacob, then Jacob, the supplanter stole it and Jacob with help from the twins' mother, Rebecca helped. Consider that God said, ***Esau have I hated, and Jacob I have loved.*** Can you imagine? A set of twins and God had to choose between the two. Esau, He hated, and Jacob was a supplanter, a thief, and a liar, but God loved him. Does that help you understand the amazing Love and forgiveness and Faith God has for mankind? That Jacob or any of us could be born so messed up and by Faith God sees us as our future selves--, our destined selves, and Loves us and helps us to get to be the self that we are supposed to be and by Grace, not passing judgment on us prematurely, although we deserve punishment for sins.

If any of us had those two as kids, twins or not, might we not be lamenting to God even about what we got in this deal? We humans look on the natural, and many times we look on the **now**. God looks on your future, finished self, and sees us through the Blood of Jesus. Oh, if we had faith and foresight like that, we would love so many more than we do.

Rebecca's Star

Men are not the only ones' born with stars. Men are not the only ones born with destinies and great destinies with lowly women as their helpers. Yes, women are called to be helpmates in Genesis, but women are also called to greatness. Hannah, Esther, Abigail, Rahab, Deborah, Ruth, Rebecca, Rachel, Mary, the mother of Jesus, Martha, Elizabeth, the mother of John the Baptist, Mary Magdalene, and so on.

And, are we not all helpers to one another?

Women of renown and great importance in Bible times and through the ages have had great stars. Without a star, how would Abraham have been able to send his servant to even find a wife for Isaac? Without a proper star and an evident, uncovered star, Rebecca would not have been found. (That's why some of you have not been *discovered*, yet; your star is covered.)

Without a star, a present and evident star how can anyone find anyone? We all have stars, and we should, else whomever is looking for you or supposed to be looking for you may be looking for a needle in a haystack. Until someone finds you, you may not be easy to see. You may just be a face in the crowd. You may be a tree in the forest—, but which tree?

It's not as though Isaac could have gone out there and gotten his own wife. Abraham wasn't letting that boy go but so far and he certainly wasn't going *clubbing* to meet new women. Princes and sons of royalty could not roam about the planet in those days. Most of all, Children of Promise were not let loose to mix with all sorts of folks. Well, it's not normally done.

I'm sure from the time on Mount Moriah when his father tied Isaac to that altar, that Child of Promise knew his dad wasn't playing. The threat, *I brought you into the world, and I can take you out*, was probably very real to Isaac.

So, if Abraham said, *You're not going out to the club, you're not going out anywhere*, Isaac stayed put. If Abraham said *It's time to get married, I'll get you a wife*, Isaac probably said, *Okay, Papa*.

Rebecca had a star and a pretty impressive one, she was to marry a prince, the son of a king; Abraham moved in a kingly and priestly anointing. Rebecca's star wasn't hidden, covered or otherwise compromised, so she was locatable. Abraham told his emissary, *There is a woman at a well, she will be doing thus and so*. The scenario was just as Abraham had said it would be. So Rebecca was located.

A woman with a star is ***seen***; she is not covered, hidden, or hiding. Abraham went on to say take her this jewelry, these earrings and this bracelet. Not only were the items gold and costly, they had a certain weight that we know was mentioned in the account. The intrinsic value of that gold was about 10K in today's markets; it was about 4 ounces of gold. But, jewelry by design is marked up quite a bit at retail, anywhere from 100% to 500%, so if Abraham had purchased that jewelry he could have paid upwards of $20K to $100K in today's market. That is the type of gift that you take a woman with a certain star, a certain future, a certain destiny. Rebecca, by destiny was marrying a prince, yet Rebecca was already by faith a queen in the eyes of the Lord and anyone else who had eyes to see and a good dose of common sense.

That she would accept, and her own family would **accept** means that she and her family and the family that was coming to wife her knew her value, they knew her worth. Else the gift and the offer may have been too paltry.

While we don't despise small or humble beginnings, don't accept miniscule offers that don't measure up to your value.

What you can be "bought" for determines your esteem, how the person who is valuating you sees you and they may forever see you that way.

For this reason, saints of God when we bring gifts and offerings to God we bring that good, acceptable, and perfect gift—the best we can to the Lord, for He is worthy. He is worthy. We want our gifts and offerings to be accepted by the King of kings. Kings, which we are, bring worthy gifts to other kings. Can you fathom bringing a trifling gift to a person of status in the natural?

An uncle traveled from overseas and brought each of his only two nephews a $2.00 key chain as a gift; cheap or not, they were ugly. Seriously? Of course, the children rejected the gifts. If a gift makes room for you and the gift is rejected, there is no special consideration given to you; you will not be regarded. In olden days, gifts were *pre*-sent, they were sent ahead of the arrival of the visitor or guest to an event such as a birthday party or wedding and if the gift was accepted then your visit or audience would be granted. If the *pre*-sent gift was rejected, you had no appointment.

Let's take this to our times and in the natural. You go on vacation—you need a hotel. You *present* your credit card when you make the reservation, else they are not going to hold that room for you. Of course, the hotel tells you ahead of time what is required for them to make room for you. If it's $279 per night, then that is what will be charged or held on your credit card so a place will be prepared for you. If you tell them to just charge or hold $50 in your card and you'll be there later with the rest-- dude, that is not happening. The "gift" has to be commensurate with where you are staying and the level of reception and accommodations that you desire and expect.

11 Brother Stars

God showed stars of Joseph's brothers bowing to him. I suppose he didn't consider Dinah a sister, or else her star had already been taken, as she had nothing to do with the Egypt debacle and the trips there to buy grain. All ten older brothers had stars.

The sun and the moon also bowed to Joseph and we deem those to be the stars of his parents.

No mention of Leah's Star, at least it did not do obeisance to Joseph in the dreams that the Lord gave him. Leah had a star, else Jacob wouldn't have accepted her, even after working 7 years for the other sister. Everybody has a star. As far as this writer is concerned, Jacob had that switcheroo coming to him after what he had done to Esau.

Rachel had a more impressive star than Leah, else Jacob wouldn't have valued her as highly as he did and work 7 more years for her. Laban, her father didn't have to trick Jacob to marry Rachel, but he pulled a fast one on Jacob to get Leah married.

Leah probably shared in the greatness of Jacob's star by association else she wouldn't have birthed heads of the Tribes of Israel, (Genesis 29:31).. Jacob bore the other heads of the Tribes of Israel with two handmaidens as well. Jacob had his own star, and it seems Jacob the Supplanter he may have had *Esau's star* as well. Come on, 12 sons, what man can do that? What man wouldn't be proud to have 12 sons?

For consideration: Ishmael became great and became a great nation because of his relationship to Abraham who also had covenant with God directly and no doubt, an impressive star, being the Father of Many Nations. Seems that anyone Abraham fathered would become *a nation.*

I am *in Abraham.*

The Star of David

The star of David is not a real thing in the Bible. There is a key of David, but the star is man's concept that has been turned into jewelry and other items. Oddly, the diagram called the Star of David looks somewhat like a pentagram, so one must be careful not to acquire or use the wrong image or depiction.

When we speak of stars, the Star of David is recognized as a symbol of Judaism, it's on the Israeli flag. In ancient times, the Star of David, called the Magen David, wasn't a Jewish symbol. It was only a common geometric symbol.

Just as our spiritual star can be covered, captured, hidden, perverted, and caused to wander, the image that we now know as the Star of David has been taken through all of that. Let's follow this meandering journey.

The oldest record of the six-point star as a Jewish symbol was around the second century. Archeologists have found Stars of David on the walls of the synagogue of Capernaum near the Sea of Galilee but think that these stars were only for décor.

Experts theorize that the star gained more meaning in Judaism in the mysterious teachings of the Kabbalah, which is it's own problem and not the scope of this book. The Book of Boundary, written in Spain in the early 14th century, contains depictions of the six-point star, which are allegedly on the Shield of David.

King David's protective shield had magical powers, they say, that could ward off *spirits* and demons. Other works of the time make similar references to the king's magical amulet with a six-point star emblazoned on it. King David was not Captain America of the comics. *We don't believe in magic, saints of God, so stay prayed up, be wise, and keep your discernment sharp.*

Roman Emperor Charles IV gave Jews who lived in Prague their own flag, it was red with a yellow Star of David on it. They were the first Jewish people to employ that star as their official emblem.

In 1897 the Star of David was chosen over the menorah as the official Zionist symbol.

To pervert the symbol of the Jewish people, Hitler decreed that all Jews under the Third Reich (1933-1945) wear a yellow six-point star as a badge of shame. The yellow Star of David is one of the most enduring images of the Holocaust.

In 1948, the star was unanimously voted to be on the flag of the State of Israel.

This Star of David, which isn't in the Bible or associated with King David in any direct way must be distinguished from a pentagram, however.

A pentagram is a symmetrical five-pointed star that appears in upright form so that one point is facing upward. Upright pentagrams have been used by many religions and cultures in history, including pagans, Christians, and Wiccans. So, you see it can be confused and conflated.

A five-pointed star has been used to symbolize the Star of Bethlehem shining over the stable where Jesus was born, and is also the shape of the stars on the American flag. The flag of Liberia has a single five-point star. Approximately 70 countries use at least one star on their flag, and it appears that 90% of those stars are 5 pointed.

Ancient Hebrews used the pentagram to represent the five books of the Torah. Symbols mean something, folks. Do your own research and we may revisit this another day, in another book.

Unlike the Star of David, modern interpretation of the pentagram is associated with evil or devil worship versus sacred religious beliefs. Satanists use an **inverted**, or upside-down pentagram as one of their symbols, while an upright pentagram is more commonly used by Wiccans. Witches get their power from whom? The devil, so this is semantics. The points of the pentagram mean earth, fire, water, air and spirit, which witches employ in their evil spells and curses.

Peace officers such as sheriffs and marshals used to design their own badges. In American frontier days badges were made out of whatever they had available. That could be anything from silver coins to lids off tin cans, hence "tin star." Although the five-pointed star is the most common of these designs, some agencies had six-, seven-, eight- or nine-point stars for badges.

Historically, and mystically, a five-pointed star supposedly imparted *magical* powers that deflected evil. A soldier wore one around his neck, believing it would protect him from enemy arrows.

Gadgets and trinkets, amulets, and jewelry, including crystals are not protective. Jesus Christ is our protection, and He gives His angels charge over us to keep us in all our ways, so we don't even stub our toe on a rock. (Psalm 91)

Jesus' Star

We do not know of the baby shower gifts Jesus' brothers and sister got. Was it not mentioned because it wasn't significant, or not *as* significant? Perhaps the brilliance of Jesus' star cast a shadow on the other children that His mother Mary gave birth to. Still, there is nothing wrong with dwelling in the Shadow of the Almighty. As a matter of fact, the Psalmist of Psalm 91 cherishes that position of safety and providence.

A baby of great *Abundance* was born in a barn or a cave and placed in the animal's feeding trough at birth. Who in their right mind would take someone with a Star of that magnitude and try to toss it in a manger as fodder for animals? Let us take note though that Jesus didn't stay in that cave. Nor did He stay in the tomb which was very much like a small cave where He was placed after being removed from the Cross after He gave up the Ghost.

Joseph and Mary went to Bethlehem on a donkey; it was a lowly animal, but it was the going mode of transport in that day. The other choice were two feet, so they weren't as poor as some think they were. I think that *poor* here may refer to the unfortunate case of having no place to shelter for the night and having to resort to a cave for the evening. Sad; *right*? Jesus did say that the Son of Man hath no place to lay His head.

As a baby, Jesus and His family went to Egypt; that takes money. Some sources say He went to India; that would take even more money. In Egypt (Africa) Jesus learned about Egyptian culture, and possibly wizardry, witchcraft. In India Jesus learned about Indian culture, and also wizardry and witchcraft. These are among the most long lasting and prevalent forms of witchcraft today. If Jesus learned about it, shouldn't we, so we will know how to pray?

As a boy, Jesus, with His Star went to the synagogue daily and taught. If 10 brothers can be jealous of Joseph, can't you imagine who all would be jealous of Jesus? Strangers usually let themselves hate freely as there is no parent saying, *Now stop; that's your brother. You two get along.*

Jesus was full of Wisdom and that is true riches; that is *Abundance*. Jesus grew more in Favor with God and man; that is *Abundance*. Jesus was full of Grace; and that is *Abundance*.

Moreover, Jesus was full of the Spirit of God and that is *Abundance* in God. Being full of the Spirit of God means Jesus was full of the Gifts of the Spirit, and that is *Abundance.*

I.   Knowledge is *Abundance*. The Word of Knowledge is one of the Gifts of the Spirit. Jesus moved in **all** the Gifts of the Spirit; that is the Christ anointing. Jesus wasn't partially gifted; He was fully gifted of God, fluent and abundant in them all.

The Word of Knowledge, a gift of the Holy Spirit is knowing something you cannot know, but you know it. Further, you **know that you know** it; you have no doubt. Not only that, the Word of Knowledge proves to be true.

II.   The gift of the **Word of Wisdom** gives the understanding of how to apply God-given Knowledge.

III.   The gift of **Faith** is given by the Holy Spirit. We are saved by Faith and we can do exploits, showing forth Signs and Wonders in the Lord, by Faith.

IV.   There are actually different kinds of healings that the Holy Spirit will do. The **Gifts of Healings** are by the Spirit of God. In His *Abundance*, Jesus moved in all of them.

V.   The Working of Miracles is when something happens that cannot be explained in the natural to bring forth deliverance, for example.

Jesus could perform miracles – not to be likened to evil miracles of the snake handler types in Pharaoh's court.

VI.   Jesus prophesied all the time. The **Gift of Prophecy** is also from the Holy Spirit is one that Scripture says *"to especially desire."*

VII.   **Discerning of Spirits** is another gift that the Holy Spirit gives to equip the discerner to see evil *spirits* operating in someone's life. I especially want to mention here that if discernment is missing but a person thinks they have the Holy Spirit, they most often don't. Please know that it is possible to have a **false holy spirit.**

A person can have the Holy Spirit but not have the gift of speaking in tongues right away. There can be many reasons for that. But if there is a false holy spirit, there can also be false tongues, as well.

Let may take this time to explain the legitimate gift of tongues which is a point of contention in the Body of Christ for no good reason.

There are three types of tongues, principally.

a. Your own heavenly or angelic language, a language between you and God. I like to call it encrypted prayer because only you and God know what you are saying. Pray in tongues to build up your most holy faith.

b. Then there is speaking in a language that you don't know but you are speaking to someone within earshot who needs to hear what thus says the Lord in the language that you are speaking, which also happens to be their language.

c. Where a Word comes through in a heavenly language and there is someone in the congregation who can properly and correctly interpret. Speaking in tongues is not done to impress people or confuse them. If no one is present to interpret, God won't have you speaking in tongues.

VIII. **The Interpretation of Tongues** is also a gift of the Holy Spirit is the ability to interpret the tongue that was spoken. This can be for yourself or the congregation. Sometimes when I am praying in tongues after I am quiet, the Holy Spirit will tell me what I just said. This is at home in my personal prayer time.

Jesus was *Abundant*, nothing missing, nothing lacking, nothing broken; He was full of *Abundance*.

When it comes to languages, Jesus most likely understood Hebrew although He probably spoke Aramaic. Jesus probably knew Greek, but it was not a common language among the people He spoke to regularly. Roman soldiers captured Jerusalem, so Latin wasn't a dead language yet. Words written on the Cross were in Latin; Jesus knew what they meant. He didn't speak Arabic because that language did not arrive in Palestine until after the first century A.D.

So, while Jesus' most common spoken language was Aramaic, he was familiar with—if not fluent, or even proficient in—three or four different tongues. As with many multilingual people, which one He spoke probably depended on the context of His words, as well as the audience He was speaking to at the time. Still, with the fullness of the Holy Spirit and all the gifts onboard, Jesus understood *everything, <u>always</u>.*

Why this is mentioned is because even now no matter what language you pray in, speak in, or hear in, the Holy Spirit knows and understands. Jesus is our Great Intercessor and some of that intercession, sometimes is interpretation. The Lord knows our heart and He knows our Words. The words we speak, they are Spirit, and they are life. Be sure to speak when you pray, else, the Lord will just be listening to your heartbeat--, since so many like to say that He knows their heart.

Star Service

We are Abraham's heirs, so some of the stars we see in the natural can be reflections of our spiritual stars. Some are ours, and some of the stars are the stars of our descendants.

One star serves another; it is not to be stolen or confiscated or sold or used by another. Just as each man is to possess his soul in sanctification and honor, let each man possess his star.

Destiny helpers have stars, too; they are not simply slaves or servants. Everyman is gifted. Stars have anointing, but they need to be protected. Pray for your star. Pray about your star. Command your star to be uncovered if you think that it is covered.

Command your star back into its proper position if you think it is wandering or lost. Cover your star with the Blood of Jesus if you think that there are or could be star hunters out there eyeing your star, or the stars of your children.

Most of all, **use** your star so it is not as an ignored or rejected star that is not being used; these are the stars that wicked hunters can snap up in a hurry. In the usage of your star God has afforded protection to you, your star, and your destiny. Do not be tricked out of your star. Also, with all that is in you, do not sin; sinning makes stars easy to steal as well.

Synergistic stars are such as two with similar stars, or even different levels of stars, but the same purpose in life may join together as Jacob did with those four women to birth those 13 children, 12 of which became the heads of the 12 Tribes of Israel. All stars will shine brighter when they are fitly joined together, as the Lord wills.

2. I soak my star and every star that
will ever come out of my bloodline
in the Blood of Jesus. Amen.

Who Is This Jesus?

Who is this Jesus with this mighty Star presence? Jesus did not come to Earth to make a name or garner fame for Himself, but with a Star like that, can it be helped? With a presence like that, can it be helped? With giftings such as Jesus carried, can that person not be noticed, in the natural? With authority like that, how could Jesus not be known both in the Spirit world and in the natural? With a Father like that, how could the *Abundance* of His firstborn son not be noticed?

In Genesis, He is the Creator. He is the Seed of the Woman. He is the Breath of Life. He is Jacob's Ladder. He is the Ark of Noah. He is the Covenant Maker. He is the Promised Redeemer.

In Exodus, He is the Burning Bush. He is the Passover Lamb.

In Leviticus He is the Tabernacle. He is the High Priest. He is the Light on the Lampstand. He is the Presence on the Mercy Seat of reconciliation. He is our Perfect Sacrifice, and He is our Thanksgiving Offering.

In Numbers, He is the Pillar of Cloud by Day and the Pillar of Fire by Night. He is Aaron's Rod that budded. He is water in the desert.

In Deuteronomy, He is the Hope of Promised Inheritance.

In Joshua, He is the Commander of the Lord's Army, the Captain of the Host of the Army of the Lord. He is the deliverer of God's people.

In Judges, He is the Judge and the Lawgiver. He is the Strength of Samson.

In Ruth, He is rest for the Weary; He is the Kinsman Redeemer.

In 1 and II Samuel, He is the Ebenezer Stone of Help. He is the Lord Saba'oth.

In Kings & Chronicles, He is the Eternal King, the Seed of David. He is the Sovereign King of kings. He is Shiloh.

In Ezra, He is the faithful Scribe.

In Nehemiah, He is the Rebuilder of the broken walls. He is the Restorer of broken people. He is the Uniter of people to work together.

In Esther He is the Advocate for His people; He is the Protector of His People and He is the Salvation of Israel.

In Job, He is the Mediator between God and man.

In Psalms, He is our Son; the Lord is our Shepherd, our High Tower and our Redeemer. He is the Lord's Right Hand. He is the King of Glory.

In Proverbs & Ecclesiastes, He is Wisdom. He is Our Strength and Our Redeemer.

In Song, He is the Rose of Sharon and the Song of songs.

In Isaiah He is the High and Lifted Up One. He is the Branch of Jesse. He is the Repairer of the Breach, and the Restorer of Paths to Dwell In. He is Wonderful, Counselor, Mighty God.

In Jeremiah and Lamentations, He is the Righteous Branch and the Restorer of Israel. He daily loads us with new mercies.

In Ezekiel, He is the Watchman. He is the God of Glory.

In Daniel, He is the Fourth Man in the fire. He is the Ancient of Days. He is the Messiah, the Coming Prince.

In Hosea, He is the faithful husband.

In Joel, He is the Spirit's power.

In Amos, He is the Everlasting Arms that carry us. He is the Tabernacle of David.

In Obadiah, He is the Judge of evil-doers.

In Jonah, He is the Great Missionary sent by God. He is the One who Rose from death to prophesy to the Lost.

In Micah He is the Promise of Peace.

In Nahum, He is our Strength and Shield.

In Habakkuk, He is the strengthener of our Faith and Trust.

In Zephaniah, He is the Warrior who Saves.

In Haggai, He is the Rebuilder and the Restorer.

In Zechariah, He is the Angel of the Lord, He is the Staff Beauty that is broken for us.

In Malachi, He is the *Abundant* Gift-giver. He is the Sun of Righteousness, with Healing in His Wings. He rebukes the devourer for our sakes.

Jesus is all that and more than we can even mention. He is Everything. Jesus came that we may have life and have it more abundantly. Jesus, full of *Abundance; He is Abundance* and He came that we might have *Him*.

The Power to Forgive Sins on Earth

Jesus has the power to forgive sins on Earth; Jesus has the power to heal. He has been given that power by spiritual giftedness to whomsoever the Father wills. Spiritual gifts are given to many, even though they are the same Gifts, there are different administrations of the Gifts.

Mankind has ever wanted to heal others–, some for altruistic reasons, some for the challenge of it, some for the power in it, some, for the money they could make from it.

Big Pharma specializes in relieving symptoms so people can keep their diseases and slow down the process of dying or ease a person into dying while their senses believe that they are okay. Sometimes Big

Pharma heals, but mostly they treat symptoms.

Jesus doesn't just dull or take away symptoms, He completely heals and takes away all traces of the disease as well as anything spiritual that would be in the aftermath of a manifesting disease.

Godly power is *Abundance*, because it is, but also because everything God gives, He gives it in *Abundance*.

Jesus Heals

Abundance can be described in terms of **authority**. Kings have more wealth than commoners or paupers. We are kings. *Abundance* follows those who can solve problems for others on Earth. *Abundance* is attracted to helpers and problem-solvers. Problem solvers solve spiritual problems by the Holy Spirit, by giftings and *authority*.

Jesus heals. Health and issues of sickness, especially those that lead to death are huge problems that humans need solved.

Often.

Jesus' *Abundance* resonates because He has authority over **every** disease symptom and disorder, whether spiritual, physical, emotional, or mental. He has authority over death, hell, and the grave. Jesus has authority over everything. When you are connected to Jesus and in relationship with Him you are in covenant with the Healer and the Restorer of our Souls.

Jesus showed the Sovereignty of God by showing His authority over EVERYTHING, all of nature, all the elements in the heavenlies, all other idols, *gods* and all diseases that they could come up with.

A disease is a sickness or malady of the body that is expressed by one or more symptom. Medicine treats symptoms and sometimes it solves them, but disease is spiritual, so the solution to spiritual problems needs to be spiritual.

Jesus rids people of the disease. Pharma, in some cases heals, but other times in essence is asking the entity causing the disease, *What can we give you that will quiet you down while you inhabit this particular body?*

Jesus said, **Suffer not a demon to speak**. Jesus shuts the demons up. Jesus casts them out, and that is when complete healing and wholeness occurs.

On deliverance ground sometimes it is useful to find out what a demon is called in order to cast it out. Once you can name a thing you can govern it. Demons sometimes play the name game; they are famous for hiding and not coming out unless you call them by their name.

Abscesses can hide, and they are dangerous. A lot of people think they are not, but a dental abscess for example can spread to other areas of the body and be very difficult to treat. If you think about it, any infection in the mouth – that close to the brain is a risk. Jesus can heal it but keep your mouth as clean as possible. Infections in the mouth impact overall health more than people realize.

Remember when God asked Ezekiel if dead bones could live? When something is dead and shriveled up, Jesus can still heal it. Jesus can unravel convoluted things and even resurrect that which is already dead. Jesus can do it all. The man with the withered hand comes to mind. Paralysis of all kinds can be healed by Jesus. It takes faith and it takes being in right relationship with Him, but you can be healed.

The Bible gives us more than one account of blindness being healed in the Bible whether they were blind from birth or not. The weather and climates in Bible locations such as sandstorms, bright sunlight and being an agrarian culture may have led to farming accidents that could have caused blindness.

Jesus can heal it all.

Job was covered at one point with boils which is a skin disease. Jesus was not walking about in flesh healing people in the Book of Job which is often considered as the first book of the Bible, but God reversed all the afflictions that the devil sent to Job. Therefore, Job was healed. We have Jesus, with Healing in His Wings, we have the Holy Spirit which is the Spirit of Deliverance to heal anything from boils to any and every other skin disorder and disease as well.

I recently saw a deliverance service where a young woman was healed of acne. This may not sound serious, but the acne infected her eye and caused blindness in one of them. Jesus heals. He has authority over that too.

Boils are usually caused by staphylococci infections (staph) and as long as the staph stays on the skin there is no problem. It is one of the reasons we also shower and bathe often to limit how much nasty stuff can build up on our skin, as well as so we don't stink, and we can keep friends. Jesus can heal even a stubborn staph infection too, but take a shower; faith without works is dead.

A carbuncle is a collection of boils. Besides being painful they are dangerous and can sometimes be fatal if not drained and treated appropriately. Recall that the plagues of Egypt included *boils*.

King Hezekiah was about to die of a boil or a carbuncle or a deep abscess. God healed Hezekiah and added 15 more years to his life. The Lord Heals.

Even with the ability to cast out demons and to heal, Jesus said to His Disciples, **Marvel not that the devils are**

subject to you, but that your name is written in Heaven.

Jesus healed deafness. In Bible environments with sandstorms and the general presence of earwax, an ear could have dirty plugs that would make a person partially or completely deaf. This is notwithstanding that a person could have been born deaf due to some middle or inner ear malformation or injury.

Spiritually, hardheaded folks who didn't listen to and heed what God was telling them were also called deaf (Isaiah 29:18). Folks, if being hardheaded runs in a family, for instance, and gets into the generations, the bloodline and the foundation, over time, deafness could be a manifestation of that hardheadedness. Things start in the spiritual realms, then over a short or long period of time they can manifest in the natural.

Jesus heals. Let Him heal your spiritual problems before they have a chance to manifest in your soul or body.

Jesus was especially known to deliver from demonic possession, such as with Legion in the Gadarenes. There is nothing that is too much for Jesus; He has authority overall. There can be no aggregation or collection of demons that can overwhelm or overpower the power of the Most High God.

Dumbness may refer to total inability to speak (mutism). The *deaf and mute spirit* is a demonic *spirit*. (Mark 7:32) This *spirit* can enter with sudden destruction, certain traumas, depression or severe stubbornness, or other traumatic brain injury (TBI).

On deliverance ground sometimes a demon that is about to be cast out will refuse to speak and sometimes has to be made to speak to identify its name, how it got there, and its reason for being there. Once you can name a thing, you can govern it.

An epileptic seizure may be anything from a slight twitch of the face or hands, or a recurring sharp, abdominal pain; this is *petit mal*. Full blown seizures are called *grand mal*. The patient suddenly falls down, loses consciousness, starts shaking all over with convulsions, chews his tongue, and foams at the mouth. The fit lasts from five to twenty minutes.

A man called to Jesus, "Lord, have mercy on my son, for he is an epileptic and suffers terribly; for often he falls into the fire, and often into the water." (Matthew 17:15) Jesus said the boy was possessed by a demon. The demon was ordered out and the boy was healed.

Fever is caused by a barrage of bacteria, virus or a parasite invading a body and that body beginning the fight to defeat and expel that offending organism. Metabolism of the body heightens and fever is the result. Usually, the body wins, and the temperature returns to normal. Jesus heals. He may heal us every night for all we know. Do any of us really know what happens every night in our sleep, in our beds? Every morning the Lord grants us new mercies. Thank You, Lord.

A woman had an issue of blood for twelve years, (Luke 8:42-48). It was a woman, so was this vaginal bleeding? Either gender could suffer dysentery and bloody diarrhea. Chronic diarrhea can be brought on by food allergies, GI diseases, abdominal surgery, long-term use of medicines, bacterial infections and parasites.

Since this was a woman with the issue of blood, this could have been brought on by fibroids--, bleeding fibroids. *Spirit spouse* turned her body into a science lab. In the natural doctors will say that this is caused by a hormone imbalance--, too much estrogen in the system. Spiritually, it is fibroids caused by *spirit husband*. Even if surgerized, fibroids often return unless *spirit spouse* has been evicted. Spiritually, *spirit spouse* is the cause of fibroids, and they are the spiritual pregnancies that prevent women from conceiving and carrying in the natural.

The Lord is our Deliverer and our Healer.

A man at the pool of Bethesda had an Infirmity 38 years. Jesus healed infirmities so severe that the infirm could either barely get to Him or couldn't get to Him at all.

Insanity, *lunatic*, madness, and mental confusion; Jesus can heal that too. (Matthew 4:24).

Leprosy was greatly feared in Bible times. Lepers were cast out of society and had to sit outside the gate. Leprosy can last 10 to 20 years, severely drain the immune system so in that time comorbidities could take a man out.

Jesus, in His Abundance, has authority over all that. Even in the Old Testament, God gave His prophets authority to heal leprosy. That dread disease still exists. Annually 200,000 are diagnosed with it in South America, Africa, and Asia with India leading the statistics and Brazil coming in second. The treatment for it is a three-antibiotic course which cures it.

Cures are inspired by and given by God who is our ultimate healer even if man has invented the meds or the course of the meds that will make a man well again. For this we thank God.

Saints of God, no matter what your diagnosis is, if you have been prescribed an antibiotic, be sure to take your antibiotics as directed and finish the courses each time, as long as you are not allergic to the meds. This is important so if you ever need that antibiotic again it will work for you as the bacteria in your body have not developed resistance to it because you stopped taking it early, such as when you felt better, or you stopped taking it because you didn't want to continue using it.

Folks, this is how vaccines work. A little bit is introduced into your system and then you develop a resistance to the disease. In the same way, when you introduce a little bit of antibiotics into your system, you develop a **RESISTANCE** to that med and it won't work for you the next time. You may not know that, however, until after the course of antibiotics is supposed to be completed and you haven't gotten any better, or you have gotten worse. Don't do that to yourself.

And don't share your meds with people; you have no idea what they are allergic to. A woman gave her 30-year-old son some of her prescription medicines to help him feel better because he came home from work saying he didn't feel well. He took the meds at mother's advice, went to bed that night and the man never woke up again. This is serious.

Yes, Jesus heals, and sometimes His way of healing is for you to go to the doctor and get a prescription, go to the pharmacist take the prescription, as prescribed, and be healed. Amen.

Be prayerful first. And if there is a simple cure for something that seems simple but might not be, then do that thing with the permission of God and your medical provider, if he or she is involved in your healing.

One year I put up a series of small flags indicating the country of origin of each of the people who worked in my office. It was a beautiful display. We had flags from so many countries. One patient looked at the display and became angry asking, *Why don't you have a flag from my country?* I thought the flags would make patients and visitors feel welcome in the setting, but not this guy, he felt the opposite of included.

At first I looked at him confused and then quickly answered, *Because you don't work here, but we accept people from all over the world.*

So, if you did not see your particular malady or ailment in the preceding lists of diseases that Jesus healed, don't become upset. Healing is anointed. The same Spirit that heals one disease can also heal another. Additionally, once you've been healed of anything, the anointing for more healing can reside in you and you can be made whole of whatever the devil throws your way, as long as you are in right standing with God. Also, what you have received you have received more than enough, so go minister to another. If you have received healing, go minister healing to another because obviously you have faith for this now. If you have received finances, go minister finances to others. That is how **Abundance** works. **Abundance** means more than enough.

Anyone attempting to store, manage or hoard **Abundance** is going against Bible teachings. **Abundance** flows, it is not stagnant. That is one of the mysteries of *Abundance*. It stands to reason that the more you give away of what you have in *Abundance*, the more you get in return.

Abundance of Christ

The *Abundance* of the Christ can be seen in how much anointing a person has and uses. A person can have anointing and do nothing with it. Faith without works is dead, but not Jesus; He abounds in Faith and also *works*. He is Omniscient, Omnipresent, Omnipotent. The many attributes and expressions of the Christ anointing reflects the *Abundance* of Jesus. The Christ anointing enables one to do all things. **ALL things.**

He grew more in stature and favor and Grace--, Favor is life.

It couldn't be stopped. Anointing, even though it is subject to the person who carries it, if that person is moving in the things of God the way God says and when God says, nothing can stop the anointed move of God.

Jesus fed the multitude with two fish & five barley loaves. The multitude of people needed to be fed, and when *Abundant* Jesus got involved, nothing could stop it.

> And Jesus took the loaves; and when he had given thanks, he distributed to the disciples, and the disciples to them that were set down; and likewise of the fishes as much as they would.
> When they were filled, he said unto his disciples, Gather up the fragments that remain, that nothing be lost.
> Therefore they gathered them together, and filled twelve baskets with the fragments of the five barley loaves, which remained over and above unto them that had eaten. (John 6:11-15)

God fills us to overflowing. Everyone had all they wanted. If you take two and add in 5, which is the number of Grace, with petition and thanksgiving, for a particular Godly purpose, **multiplication** –

abundant multiplication resulted. God had said in Genesis: Be fruitful and multiply.

Nothing could stop it. Jesus came that we may have life and nothing could stop it.

If you look at some of the things that Jesus' human side of His family went through, it's a miracle that Jesus was ever born. Abraham was worried that he'd die twice at the hand of an Abimelech, so he lied that Sarah was not his wife. Isaac almost got sacrificed on Mount Moriah. Isaac also lied to an Abimelech about Rebecca being his wife. Jacob and Esau's fights were epic. Jacob's children were outrageous. Judah, the line that Jesus came from--, none of them were perfect.

The same could be said of you, or I – any of us.

Nothing could stop Jesus' arrival here on Earth. Then nothing could stop Jesus' ministry, try as they may. Only the prophetic Word and the appointed time appeared to stop His ministry, but the ministry of Jesus is still going on. Nothing could stop it because of the *Abundance* of

Jesus. Because of the *Abundance* of His anointing, and because of the *Abundance* of His Father's riches in Glory.

You were born. You have no idea what warfare was involved in that. You came to Earth for a purpose. See to it. Do it. You, too are charged to be fruitful and multiply--, even to *Abundance*. This does not just mean having kids or earning money, but in all the ways that a life should be abundant, you should be enjoying that. In Christ, let nothing stop you.

Even on the Cross, because of the *Abundance* in Jesus' Blood, nothing can stop Him and in Faith, nothing can stop anyone who is *in Him.*

Saints, as Jesus came to fulfill the Law, everything that is a Law in the Old Testament, not only did He fulfill it--, He is still fulfilling it because He is a Godly altar, He is abundant, and He is eternal.

The Pentateuch includes the first five books of the Hebrew Bible: Genesis, Exodus, Leviticus, Numbers, and Deuteronomy. These are called the Books of the Law, the Pentateuch of the Torah.

Jesus came to fulfill the Law, not to do away with it. Be Fruitful and Multiply is a commandment that is still valid. He was the firstborn of many brethren, He came here for us, and he allowed himself to be broken until He bled, for us. In us, through us, we are now many brethren, where Jesus has multiplied Himself.

The fishes and the loaves was one of only a few "offerings" I saw that Jesus ever received in the Gospels. And when He prayed over it--, Lord, have Mercy--, it was so much more than enough. That's *Abundance.*

In the Old Testament there was a widow woman who met up with Elijah, she did according to instruction and there was food every day for Elijah, the woman and her household. The jar of flour was not exhausted, and the jug of oil did not run dry. Elijah ministered multiplication and thereby, *Abundance* according to the Word of the Lord.

Jesus came to fulfill the Law. Not to do away with it.

Again, the Old Testament, there was another widow that needed money so that her sons wouldn't be sold into slavery (2 Kings 4). The prophet, Elisha asked her, *What do you have in the house?*

She answered, *A little oil.*

The prophet told her to go borrow jars, and do not gather just a few. This prophet knew that if God was going to minister it would be in *Abundance*.

The prophet told her to then go inside, shut the door behind you and your sons and pour oil into all the jars you have borrowed. The oil did not stop until the woman ran out of jars. God is all about *Abundance* and He put Abundance in Jesus. We are in Christ therefore we should all be abundant in all we say and do.

However, know that you will be fully vetted by God so you are not random and reckless and become evil and selfish, saying and doing evil things knowingly or unknowingly because God has given you power and authority. *In Christ* means not leaning on your own understanding, in your flesh, or doing just what you want to do. You must be *in Christ.*

You see, nothing can stop the Word of God that is in action. Once faith is in action, nothing can stop it and nothing should be able to stop you. Once you are speaking the Word of God, you are asking things properly, you are moving things, nothing will be able to stop you. If you are *in Christ* and He is in you, since nothing can stop Him, then nothing should be able to stop you.

Every knee will bow, every tongue will confess that Jesus is Lord. Nothing resists God.

Once Jesus broke the bread and the fish and put them on the Godly altar, *with thanksgiving*, the altar started multiplying.

When we are in Christ we are in His realm. Everything that happens for Christ should happen for us when we are in His realm (Colossians 1:27). When you pray a thing, in the Name of Jesus, it shall be done for you. When two agree as touching, you can have what you ask for. Be sure to ask correctly and in faith for the right purposes.

The only things that can stop it are man not fulfilling the requirements of coming to God in the first place or asking correctly. Things such as Doubt. Unbelief. Asking amiss. Selfish requests. Sin can stop it, but that's all on you. If you are in right order with the Lord, you cannot be stopped.

There is no condemnation in Christ, our thoughts can't be condemned, we can't be condemned, our words cannot be condemned, our prayer requests cannot be condemned. There is no condemnation for those who are **in** Christ Jesus.

Multiplication leads to *Abundance*. We should be multiplying ourselves for the Kingdom of God. You are someone to God, with your beautiful star, so whatever we touch should prosper.

As the Lord pours out His Spirit on all flesh, we will be more and more like Jesus, moving in *Abundance* to the Glory of God. Be fruitful and multiply: Jesus did that and showed us how to do it.

3. Lord, if I'm 70% water, come to my wedding feast and turn that water into wine, in the Name of Jesus.
4. Lord, turn that water into gladness and joy, in the Name of Jesus.
5. Lord, turn that water into covenant making liquid, in the Name of Jesus.
6. Lord, turn that water into spirit, Holy Spirit that all who drink will declare this is the best ever, it is better than the first, in the Name of Jesus.

Divorce Poverty

There are statisticians who report on whether poverty affects divorce.

It does.

I ask does divorce affect poverty levels of individuals and families? And, the answer is, Yes, it affects that too.

Statistics in the USA show that Marital Status & Poverty indicated that nearly more than 40% of widows are considered impoverished but the poverty rate for married people is about 30%. Divorced before age 50 is 15 to 20% whereas married and never divorced the poverty rate is only around 3%.

I've been telling you, get married, stay married and be satisfied with the spouse of your youth. Never married poverty stats are at 12%. Disproportionately, 27% of single women, divorced before age 50 are considered poor or in poverty.

Be fruitful and multiply. I wrote an entire book on this because of its importance. More than once I've spoken about how divorce is *un-multiplication*.

Somone recently said to me that not getting married is different than getting divorced with the implication that getting divorced needs serious or more serious prayer treatment than not ever getting married. I will agree with that on one condition: that the unmarried is celibate and not burning sexually or committing sex sins. Then I'll agree that the unmarried is called to be unmarried and does not need prayer or deliverance from being single.

Jesus was not married.

Nor was He divorced.

Neither of those things were in His ministry mandate. We are not Jesus, but we follow Him as He does what He sees the Father do.

Multiplication leads to **Abundance**. *Un*-multiplication shuts down the track that leads to **Abundance**. Jesus was abundant in not ever getting married because He was upright before the Lord and celibate. If we commit sexual sins, we become unstable and unblessed, in the order of Reuben. Also, our blessings may be withheld or diverted because of sin and iniquity.

Disunity, dissensions, division--, either all these attitudes, *spirits* and problems promote poverty, or travel with the *spirit of poverty.*

7. Lord, I divorce poverty and have poverty divorce me, on the grounds of irreconcilable differences, then let it be, in the Name of Jesus.

Abundance of Jesus

How can you minister what you don't have? We are ever looking at people's results, reviews and accomplishments, even online to decide if we will patronize their restaurant or business. Who wants a football coach who has never played football? Who wants to go to a restaurant and pay top dollar for an unproven chef? Nope, people want to see awards, certificates, diplomas--, results.

How can you minister what you don't have and not covet it for yourself? Jesus ministered health and healing; there is no record of Jesus ever having been sick. Jesus ministered life resurrecting more than one; and to one, more than once. Jesus Himself would be resurrected, Amen. Jesus ministered *Abundance*; He sent the two Disciples to get the coin from the fish's mouth; He didn't say oh, there's money oh wow, go get that for Me and bring it to Me.

Jesus had a treasurer. Do poor people have a treasurer? Do they have a bookkeeper, an accountant, or a CPA?

A person who has never seen money before and is fascinated with money, even to the point of worship of Mammon keeps their money on them, with them, in eyesight at all times. They don't have a treasurer. Some don't even put their money in a bank. Nope, it is with them, or as close to them as possible at all times. Where your heart is, there is also your treasure.

People who argue that Jesus was poor are so mistaken. Frankincense, incense, and gold were His baby shower gifts. Did you get gifts like that as a baby? Maybe some of you did. Have you ever given gifts such as that to a newborn? Maybe some of you have, but it is not the norm.

Many estimate that at that time, translated into modern money, frankincense would have cost $500 per pound. Myrrh would have cost $4,000 per pound. While much is known about the gifts themselves, the bearers, known as the Magi or "Wise Men," remain somewhat mysterious to modern scholars.

It's absurd to think that wealthy sages would travel across the desert for weeks, if not months, or years to bring the Christ child $2.00 key chains. No, they brought **treasures**. A small chest of gold, approximately less than 8″ inches square would weigh over 50 pounds, would be an appropriate gift for a king. Today's market value for gold is about $2,500/troy ounce and with 12 troy ounces per troy pound a 50-pound box of gold would be valued at about 1.5 million dollars.

Frankincense and myrrh were even more valuable than gold during the time of Christ. Although we don't know how much the Magi gave, if we estimate that their gifts were of comparable value, then the combined gifts would be worth three to five million dollars.

King Herod did not seem to be concerned about prophecies of a male child being born until wealthy and influential

Magi and their retinue, from the EAST came looking to "worship" Jesus then he sat up and took notice. Why else would Herod have tried to kill Jesus as a baby? Was he really concerned that a baby would take over his kingdom, or could it be that he was after the great wealth that the Magi brought as gifts? Herod didn't send killers after the Magi or the army that was allegedly with them. No, Herod sent killers looking for baby Jesus and, in the process, put a hit on all male children under 2 years old.

The *spirit of Herod* is still in this Earth today. Saints of God, you'd better stay prayed up.

A very wealthy Christian commissioned a team of historians to research the Magi and the gifts they brought to Jesus when he was born. Their conclusion was that more than 300 kings came bearing gifts for Jesus, with an estimated wealth of $5 million. It is said that Persian documents showed that the gift was escorted by an army.

Oh, this would have really gotten Herod's attention and ire.

After Jesus was born in Bethlehem in Judea, during the time of King Herod, Magi from the east came to Jerusalem and asked, "Where is the one who has been born king of the Jews? We saw his star when it rose and have come to worship him." (Matthew 2:2)

Herod ordered all of the male children under the age of two years old to be killed. Joseph and Mary, with Jesus escaped to Egypt to save Jesus' life. Being able to escape death, to escape war, even if you are the only or one of the targets takes *Abundance*. War against 2-year-olds is war against families. All families are not able to escape war-torn countries; it takes finances.

If it is true that Jesus was born into a poor family, He did not remain poor--, I mean the baby shower was a big hit, if He was still a baby. If He was two years old by then, and his birthday party had a bouncy house--, if those gifts were converted to money--, gifts such as gold, frankincense, and myrrh, that bouncy house would have been **filled** with money.

Jesus' Star alone foretold great wealth and *Abundance* amongst other gifts which we now know are the true riches.

Holy Spirit is telling me here that Jesus did not have the tendency to sell Gifts that He received. We take this into the New Testament when the woman with the alabaster box of precious ointment broke it and poured it on His feet. Judas said they could have sold that ointment; Jesus said something else entirely. People who are used to wealth and *Abundance* don't sell sentimental things, they don't sell appropriate gifts very quickly, often, and sometimes not at all. They also don't consume gifts right away but by Wisdom may hold on to them until the appointed time for use. In the Bible it was against the law to sell something that you had inherited, such as land.

Abundant people *give* to others more often than they sell. This is not to say that an abundant person cannot be a businessman. I believe God loves businesspeople.

But in the Kingdom of God we say, freely I have received; freely I give.

There are people with spiritual gifts who are demanding a price for prayers and deliverance--, better check with God on this to be sure they are *of God*. Jesus didn't ask for money or an offering to heal or deliver. Stay prayerful, dear readers.

Ho, every one that thirsteth, come ye to the waters, and he that hath no money; come ye, buy, and eat; yea, come, buy wine and milk without money and without price. (Isaiah 55:1)

Buy the truth, and sell it not; also wisdom, and instruction, and understanding. (Proverbs 23:23)

The Abundant *Give*

The ***Abundant*** Messiah cannot help but minister ***Abundance***, the only requirement is that He first must see that you are ready to receive net-breaking, boat-sinking increase so that you have more than enough to fulfill what He has called you to do.

God would not let something flow through you and not let you experience that something as well. When you give Mercy, you receive Mercy. When you give Grace, you receive Grace. When you pray for others; you receive—it's a spiritual law.

On the negative side the pit you dig for another becomes your pit. When you are hateful, you get hate—you reap what you sow. When you give money; you get money or something else of value. When you give

Abundance, you receive *Abundance*. Jesus always gives abundantly.

When you put something on an altar, it interfaces with the spiritual world – depending on what altar and what kind of altar. What you put on an altar, in faith, connects to the spiritual realms, multiplies and goes where it is intended to go.

If it is a Godly altar, you do all that, but you don't lose anything. He that would lose his life will save it. It's back to my *copy and paste* analogy. You put something on an altar, and it is copied, but like a copy demand in your computer software, it is copied, but it is still there. Now on an altar a thing is considered consumed, and you don't repent of having sown it, but now that thing placed on the altar is in the Spirit and *Spirit don't* die. It doesn't die, it multiplies. Not only does it multiply, it now sprouts wings and it can go withersoever you send it, withersoever the Lord commands it, wherever it should go.

Things can remain on Earth, in the Earth and die like flesh, or they can be put in the Spirit and bear fruit that remains and Live. Amen.

The Words I speak, they are Spirit, and they are Life. What is put on an altar multiplies. That works both ways – a Godly altar multiplies Godly things for Godly results. An evil altar multiplies evil. Saints of God be sure you know what altar you are sacrificing on every time you make an offering or pay a sacrifice. One must also have faith in **Who** is backing that altar.

Jesus knew that; Jesus automatically did that and not only lived in *Abundance* in every way, but ministered it to others. When you are speaking, sharing, telling, or teaching, the first thing that most people want to know, silently or boisterously is, *On what authority are you speaking to me?*

Jesus was given **all authority** from the Father, but people have to see that authority, believe in that authority and respect it to receive what the person is ministering.

And Jesus came and spoke to them, saying, "All authority has been given to

Me in heaven and on earth.
(Matthew 28:18)

Just as the plagues of Egypt strategically attacked and defeated the main idol *gods* of that land when God was bringing the Hebrews out of Egypt, I believe Jesus sought out certain ailments to heal. He knew by a Word of Knowledge where those diseases/demons would be in the ones that sought Him out to demonstrate the power of God.

Messiah demonstrated His authority and power. Authority in the spirit translates to authority in the natural. That translates to power and power is ***Abundance***. Show me any weak person who is abundant. One must be powerful in something, or an authority in at least one thing to wield any type of power. Or, be in connection with the strength of the entity backing the altar that they are serving. Jehovah.

My Bible says I can do ALL things through Christ. That makes me anointed, appointed, authorized, powerful and abundant. I have the Spirit of God and the Mind of Christ; I can do all things through Christ which strengthens me. Amen. If

Jesus has been given all authority and I can do all things in Him, then that's where you'll find me--, in Christ and also in *Abundance*.

In the case of healing, the devil causing the disease is cast out--, that is, sent away. Devils are not meant to be in humans, not in their soul or their bodies, they cause a lot of malfunctions, including illness, sickness, and death. The abundant man is not ill or sick, or diseased or disordered physically, emotionally, nor mentally.

Jesus has authority over everything that He has mastered. All captivity He took captive, He still has authority over it.

So, while you are captive and sitting in some demonic prison, Jesus has authority over the demons that believe they have authority over you. Why have you not mentioned His Name yet? Why have you not called *time*? Why have you not said, that there is one Greater whose shoelaces you are not fit to loosen; and as a matter of fact that is where you are, you devils, you are at His feet where His shoelaces actually are.

He IS

In Matthew He is God with us. He is Messiah who is King.

In Mark, He is the Miracle Worker. He is the Messiah who is Servant.

In Luke, He is the son of Mary, He is the Messiah who Delivers.

In John, He is the Word, He is Messiah, He is the Lamb of God and the Bread of Life. He is the Light of the World, the Good shepherd and the Resurrection and Life, He is the Way, the Truth, and the Life.

In Acts, He is the indwelling Spirit.

In Romans, He is the Righteousness of God. He is the Law and Grace that sustains us.

In 1 Corinthians, He is Love.

In 2 Corinthians, He is the Patience of God.

In Galatians He is our Life.

In Ephesians, He is the Head of the Church, He is the Unity of the Body.

In Philippians, He is the Peace of God.

In Colossians: He is the Supreme Ruler over all. He is the Glory in us, He is the Godhead, He is the Trinity.

In 1 & 2 Thessalonians, He is the Comfort in the Last Days and He is the Coming King.

In Timothy, Titus and Philemon, He is the Foundation of Truth, He is Faithful Pastor and Mediating Priest.

In Hebrews, He is our High Priest, Ever-Present God, the Captain of our Salvation. He is the author and Finisher of our Faith.

In James, He is the Healing we need.

In 1 Peter, He is the Bishop of our souls. He is the Chief Shepherd.

In 2 Peter He is our Example (our supermodel)

In 1, 2, and 3 John, He is True Love.

In Jude, He is our protector from falling.

In the Revelation, He is the King of kings and the Lord of lords. He is Alpha and Omega. He is the Beginning and the End. He is the Maker of all things new.

In Life, He is *all that* and more. He is *Abundance*.

Jesus Takes Away

Jesus takes away the sin of the world. Not only that, He takes away all the residual--, the yokes and the bondages, and iniquity of that sin. Jesus is not our trashman, but when you take out the trash at home, sometime the bag may break or leak and there's a trail of something liquid that probably never should have been put in that bag and it makes a mess on the floor. If that trash is sin that is being removed from a person's life, then that trail that follows after it is iniquity. And, it can lead to a trail of tears.

Man was not made for sin; but sin was made for man. Man was made to serve and worship God, not for sin or any residual of sin.

Even if nothing leaks out in a solid form, sometimes garbage can smell so foul that there is a reeking odor in the air; that's iniquity. The smell of sin is more appropriate because both smell and iniquity are invisible.

The visitation of God upon the iniquity is not invisible, it can be physical and palpable. Iniquity is invisible because after sinning and nothing seems to happen, most humans think they got away with it; but they didn't. Unless repented of quickly, not repeated, and the iniquity was not removed, it will follow like the wake of a speedboat. There is always a wake.

The Lord giveth; He giveth Life, he giveth Mercy, He giveth Truth, and He giveth *Abundance*.

The Lord taketh away--, the sin of the world **and** the iniquity associated with sin.

Blessed be the Name of the Lord.

Prayers for *Abundance*

You've heard the saying, *You can't get there from here,* right? We could pray prayers for **Abundance,** but we need to pray that prayer from a place where we can get to **Abundance**. Of course, God can do anything He wants, and God can change a life, a wallet, or a bank account overnight, or even in a moment. A lot of that is based on your faith--, if you believe you can get there from where you are, then Hallelujah!

If the pastor, the prophet, or God Himself tells you the new thing He's going to do in your life, but you have no faith for it, then it just won't happen. God won't force goodness on you. Saints, when you have a prophetic dream or a prophetic

Word, you have to do something about it—
pray it through.

Conversely the devil forces evil on people all the time. So, if you have upcoming information that the devil is planning something nefarious against you, then you'd better pray fervently and perhaps also with fasting as Wisdom and the Word and Spirit of God instructs.

To get to *Abundance* perhaps you need to first get **from** lack and insufficiency to at least sufficiency and understand how to live there **first**. Perhaps you experience sufficiency for only one day, or one week, or one month, but you learn sufficiency first. Learn, feel, and know what it's like in the provision of the Lord. This affects and prospers your soul.

Now we believe in miracles, and sometimes we need a miracle. Do you have faith for a miracle? Then Praise God!

8. Lord, let me never be in desperation, in the Name of Jesus.

9. Lord, bring me into Abundance and bring Abundance to me, in Jesus' Name.

10. Father, if my journey to Abundance is sudden or sequential, let it be according to Your plans for my life, but do not let it tarry, and redeem the time for me, in Jesus' Name.

We want *Abundance*? That most often comes with coming out of poverty and out of lack and living in sufficiency while honoring God. We don't serve or worship Mammon, we pay tithes and give offerings, we deal properly with our own money. We deal properly with others as we deal with money, and we deal properly with others as we deal properly with *their* money.

Exercising the disciplines is how your faith is built up and where God can command the blessing. Where there is unity, there God commands the blessing. Where you have joined in with God and His Word, you have become one with God, walking in step with Him; there He commands the blessing.

The blessings of God are always big, they are more than enough; they are abundant. Jesus said, I **do what I see My Father do. The Father and I are ONE**. Now you see how God commanded the blessing on Jesus and why Jesus was abundant in everything He did.

11. Lord, bring me out of lack and insufficiency, in the Name of Jesus.
12. Jehovah Jireh, You are my Provider; bring me to the place of enough that I can neither embarrass You or be brought to shame, in the Name of Jesus.
13. Lord, bring me out of poverty, and bring poverty out of me, in the Name of Jesus.
14. Father, where I have left my first estate, restore me, in the Name of Jesus.
15. Lord, restore the years, restore the time, restore to me what the cankerworm and the palmerworm have eaten, in the Name of Jesus.
16. Lord, restore to me all that the devourer has devoured, have him

vomit it out again, in the Name of Jesus.

17. Lord, every blessing that has been swallowed, let that power retch and retch until it is *un*-swallowed, in the Name of Jesus.

18. Lord, let me be one with You and there command the blessing, in the Name of Jesus.

19. Lord, let me hear the sound of the *Abundance* of rain, even showers of blessing, in the Name of Jesus.

20. Lord, command Goodness, Favor, and Mercy over my life, in the Name of Jesus.

21. Lord, let both me and my enemies see Your Hand of favor and *Abundance* over all of my life, in the Name of Jesus.

22. Lord, bring health and healing to every part of my body, soul, and spirit and reveal to me the *Abundance* of Your Peace and Truth, in the Name of Jesus.

23. Jesus Christ has redeemed me from the Curse of the Law; I am

redeemed from poverty, sickness and death into the *Abundant* Life, in the Name of Jesus.

24. I am *in Christ*. I am **one** with Christ. Lord, let the Christ anointing fall on me so there is no place for sickness, disease, disorder, or death, in the Name of Jesus.

25. Lord, let the anointing of *Abundance* fall on my life so that I am prospered, healthy, joyful, complete, and satisfied in every way, in the Name of Jesus.

26. Lord, satisfy me with good things, in the Name of Jesus.

27. The blessings of the Lord, maketh rich, and He addeth no sorrow with it, in the Name of Jesus.

28. I seal these prayers, decrees and declarations with the Blood of Jesus and the Spirit of Promise over every dimension, age, era and timeline, past, present and future, to infinity, in the Name of Jesus.

29. Any backlash because of this Word, these prayers and these decrees and

declarations backfire against the sender, to infinity, in the Name of Jesus.

AMEN.

Dear Reader

Thank you for acquiring and reading this volume. I pray God's *Abundance* will fill every part of your life and into your generations that you all live until you are satisfied, that you be fruitful and multiplied, and that God be glorified,

In the Name of Jesus.

Dr. Marlene Miles

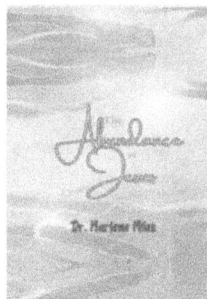

Prayer books by this author

While most books by this author have prayer points either throughout the book or at the end, there are some books that are **only** prayers. You just open up the book and pray. They are listed below:

Prayers Against Barrenness: *For Success in Business and Life*

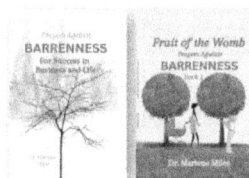

Fruit of the Womb: *Prayers Against Barrenness*

Beauty Curses, *Warfare Prayers Against*
https://a.co/d/5Xlc2OM

Courts of Marriage: Prayers for Marriage in the Courts of Heaven *(prayerbook)*
https://a.co/d/cNAdgAq

Courtroom Warfare @ Midnight
(prayerbook) https://a.co/d/5fc7Qdp

Demonic Cobwebs *(prayerbook)*
https://a.co/d/fp9Oa2H

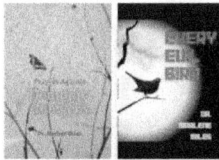

Every Evil Bird https://a.co/d/hF1kh1O

Every Evil Arrow https://a.co/d/afgRkiA

Gates of Thanksgiving

Soulish & Diabolical Prayer Treatments

https://a.co/d/idFDOOp

Spirits of Death & the Grave, Pass Over
Me and My House
https://a.co/d/dS4ewyr

*Please note that my name is spelled incorrectly on
amazon, but not on the book.*

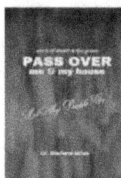

Throne of Grace: Courtroom Prayer

https://a.co/d/fNMxcM9

Warfare Prayer Against Poverty
https://a.co/d/bZ611Yu

Other books by this author

Abundance of Jesus, *The*

AK: *The Adventures of the Agape Kid*

AMONG SOME THIEVES

Ancestral Powers https://a.co/d/9prTyFf

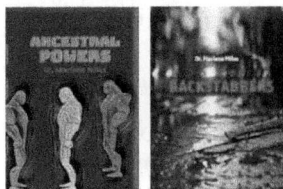

Backstabbers https://a.co/d/gi8iBxf

Barrenness, *Prayers Against*
https://a.co/d/feUltIs

Battlefield of Marriage, *The*

Blindsided: *Has the Old Man Bewitched You?* https://a.co/d/5O2fLLR

Break Free from Collective Captivity

Casting Down Imaginations
https://a.co/d/1UxlLqa

Church *Craft: Witchcraft In the Church*

Churchzilla, The Wanna-Be, Supposed-to-be Bride of Christ

Curses of Blind Men

Demonic Cobwebs (prayerbook)

Demonic Time Bombs

Demons Hate Questions

Devil Loves Trauma, *The*

Devil Weapons: Unforgiveness, Bitterness,…

The Devourers: Thieves of Darkness 2

Do Not Swear by the Moon

Don't Refuse Me, Lord (4 book series)
https://a.co/d/idP34LG

Dream Defilement

The Emptiers: *Thieves of Darkness, 1*
https://a.co/d/5I4n5mc

Every Evil Arrow https://a.co/d/afgRkiA

Evil Touch https://a.co/d/gSGGpS1

Failed Assignment
https://a.co/d/3CXtjZY

Fantasy Spirit Spouse
https://a.co/d/hW7oYbX

FAT Demons (The): *Breaking Demonic Curses*

The Fold (5-book series)

- The Fold (Book 1)
- Name Your Seed (Book 2)

- The Poor Attitudes of Money (3)
- Do Not Orphan Your Seed (4)
- For the Sake of the Gospel (5)
- My Sowing Journal

Gang Ups: Touch Not God's Anointed

got HEALING? Verses for Life

got LOVE? Verses for Life

got HOPE? Verses for Life

got money? https://a.co/d/g2av41N

How to Dental Assist

How to Dental Assist2: Be Productive, Not Wasteful

I Take It Back

Legacy

Let Me Have A Dollar's Worth
https://a.co/d/h8F8XgE

Level the Playing Field

Living for the NOW of God

Lose My Location
https://a.co/d/crD6mV9

Man Safari, *The*

Marriage Ed. Rules of Engagement & Marriage

Made Perfect in Love

Money Hunters: Beware of Those

Money on the Altar https://a.co/d/4EqJ2Nr

Mulberry Tree https://a.co/d/9nR9rRb

Motherboard (The) ~ *Soul Prosperity Series*

Name Your Seed

Occupy: *Until I Return*

Plantation Souls

Players Gonna Play

Power Money: Nine Times the Tithe
https://a.co/d/gRt41gy

The Power of Wealth *(forthcoming)*

Powers Above

Repent of Visiting Evil Altars
https://a.co/d/3n3Zjwx

The Robe, Part 1, The Lessons of Joseph

The Robe, Part II, The Lessons of Joseph

Seasons of Grief

Seasons of Waiting

Seasons of War

Second Marriage, Third~~, *Any Marriage*

https://a.co/d/6m6GN4N

Sift You Like Wheat

Six Men Short: What Has Happened to all the Men?

Soul Prosperity soul prosperity series 3

https://a.co/d/5p8YvCN

Souls Captivity soul prosperity series 2

The Spirit of Poverty

StarStruck

SUNBLOCK

The Swallowers: *Thieves of Darkness*, 3

Take It Back

This Is NOT That: How to Keep Demons from Coming at You

Time Is of the Essence

Too Many Wives: *Why You Have Lady Problems*

Tormenting Spirits   https://a.co/d/dAogEJf

Toxic Souls

Triangular Power *(series)*

- Powers Above
- SUNBLOCK

- Do Not Swear by the Moon
- STARSTRUCK

Uncontested Doom

Unguarded Hours, *The*

Unseen Life, *The* https://a.co/d/0drZ5Ll

Upgrade: How to Get Out of Survival Mode

- Toxic Souls (Book 2 of series)
- Legacy (Book 3 of series)

The Wasters: *Thieves of Darkness*, Bk 2
https://a.co/d/bUvI9Jo

What Have You to Declare? What Do You Have With You from Where You've Been?

When I Was A Child, *I Prayed As a Child*

When the Devourer is Rebuked

https://a.co/d/1HVv8oq

The Wilderness Romance *(series)* This series is about conducting a Godly relationship and marriage with someone who is a Wilderness person. It is about how to recognize it and navigate through it. These books are about how not to get caught up in such.

- *The Social Wilderness*
- *The Sexual Wilderness*
- *The Spiritual Wilderness*

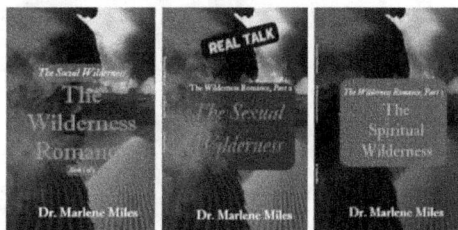

Other Series

Spirit Spouse books

https://a.co/d/9VehDSo

https://a.co/d/97sKOwm

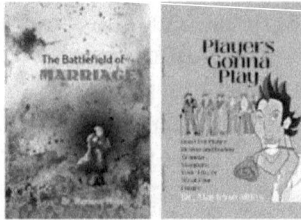

Thieves of Darkness series

Triangular Powers https://a.co/d/aUCjAWC

Upgrade (series) *How to Get Out of Survival Mode* https://a.co/d/aTERhXO